Fragments of a Life

A Collection of Poems

Judith A. Rucki

No Frills
<<<>>>
Buffalo
Nofrillsbuffalo.com

Pages 13, 21, 33, 39, 45, 59, 65, 85, 89 93, 103, 107;
photographs by Jill Pogodzinski

Pages 21, 39, 59, 85, 89, 93; modeled by Abigail
Militello

Printed in the United States of America

Fragments of a Life/ Rucki- 1st Edition
ISBN: 978-0615540313

No Frills Buffalo
<<<>>>
119 Dorchester
Buffalo, NY 14213

Visit nofrillsbuffalo.com

Dedication

This book is dedicated to …

My parents, Alphonse and Harriet Rucki, who spent many hours reading to me and sharing their love of the written word … and …

My husband, Martin Pipolo, for his continued support, generosity and reminders to, "Stop worrying and enjoy life!"

4

Foreword

In our day to day, there are words that
quietly spring to mind
-- passages writ to set the time.
Such is it for the journey of Judith
-- the being alive with the nuances of
perception ...
the gathering up of self in the smallest
gestures of reality.
I thank Judith for letting me see her poems.
There is still an image in my mind -- herself
-- a young girl
-- a budding young woman peering at me
over her books,
pencil in hand, through her long dark hair.
So I come back years later -- cherish that
image and the depth reached to where
grows her soul to breathe experience.

C.M. Butterick

Introduction

I've loved stories and poems for as long as I can remember. My mother read to me so often I knew many children's books by heart. Some of my earliest memories are of my father reading the Sunday comics to me. My Aunt Helen Krzyzykowski gave me free reign in her library, where I discovered the classics, along with whatever was on the best seller list at the time.

My parents and my aunt gave me great gifts … they taught me how to read and granted access to publications worth reading.

Books have been my constant companions. Rheumatic fever, contracted when I was age 10, often left me too tired to run around and play, but never too worn out to read. I was able to travel to distant lands, imagine the future and partake of adventures without ever leaving my room.

In my professional life I spent many years writing and editing newspapers, newsletters, brochures, ad copy, news releases, white papers, speeches and articles. I labored in the corporate, non-profit and higher education worlds, each presenting a different set of challenges and rewards.

At one point I taught a college course in Public Relations Writing. It was easy to see who enjoyed the craft as much as I did, and it was a delight to watch talent blossom.

Poetry, for me, was never a means to earning a living, but creating it has been nourishment for the soul. The work in this "slim volume" is the result of more than 40 years worth of writing. The poems aren't necessarily products of my experience. Some of them came to me in dreams, some as random thoughts and others as a result of stories told by family and friends.

I liken this book to a peach. It starts out green, moves into the ripe, juicy years and ends up a little over-ripe but still sweet. Indeed it is fragments of a life … some belonging to me, the rest belonging to beloved family and friends who have been a part of this journey.

In the Beginning

Blessings

I want to hear your stories
In great, deadly detail.
Unravel the mysteries slowly
And tell me everything I missed
Over the many decades
I remained pressed against
Your great silence.
The years tumble backward
And forward once again.
I once missed feeling
The rhythm of your days.
I am grateful you accepted my offer
Of imperfect love.

Just Us

There's a certain comfort
Attached to walking into a room
And watching a sea
Of prematurely gray heads turning
And myopic pale blue eyes
Staring back
At one of their own.
We take our places
The scientists on this side
Artists on the other.
Mingling at the weddings and funerals
That come so rarely
And then too often.
What is our legacy?
Did something drive us apart
Or did we simply drift
Away from each other?
One of us laughs.
Doesn't matter which one.
We share the same voice.

Thoughts of Ancient Evenings

I read your words
Carefully
Then again.
I was beyond picturing
The lush gardens
Flowing rivers
Crowded market places
You so beautifully depicted.
It was more like
I remembered
Somewhere in time
Sailing down the Nile
Watched the pyramids
Take shape
As slaves labored
Under the merciless sun.
I watched the preparations
Right up until
The moment
I was buried with my pharaoh
(Or was he a king?)
In case he needed attending
On the other side.
Where is he now?
What is my purpose
So many thousands of years
And miles
Away from the land
That once, surely
Was mine, too?

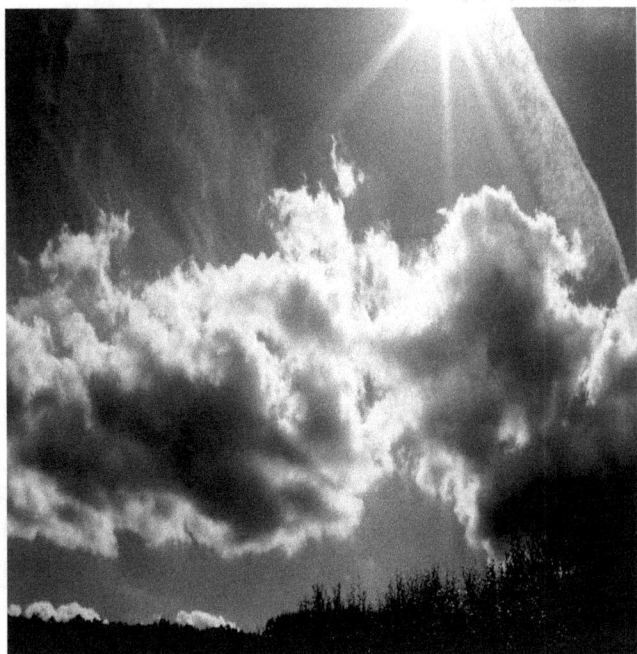

Ancient Lore

What drew us to
This land, this garden,
The open space
We called our own?
How is it we share
The ability to draw
The native faces
Carve the symbols
Into old stones
Cry out to horses
We remember riding
In another place
Another century?
Is this some reincarnation
That links us to
The warriors
We feel live on
In our blood, our bones?
None of us can explain
But we see it
In each others' eyes.
Looking off into the distance
We watch the smoke
We read our story.
Then we tell it again.
If only to each other.

Women of the Earth

They were my grandmothers, my aunts
My mother
Solid, earthbound, adept
At bringing forth life from the earth.
I see them
Plucking fruit from the trees they planted
Carrying ripe offerings in faded aprons
Kneading dough with fingers made strong
From connecting to the soil, the earth.
Creating, feeding, nurturing us
Truly the fruit of their labors.

The Men

The men in our family
Were simple enough
In a good way.
They simply knew
What to do
How to do it
And, bless them,
They did it.
Even when they were very young,
Not yet considered men
Of or by the world
They took up
The tools of their trade
Or arms in defense
Of home and country.
Whatever needed tending
They got it done
Without really thinking
Much about it.
Asked if they were happy
With their work
Their lives
They would say
There were no questions
To be asked
Or answered.
The work was completed
The battle won
The country saved
The family safe.
They were plainspoken
Wise, perhaps
And world weary
Beyond their years.

And always
They were men.

Stillborn

They said he was my brother
At least I got to see him
Unlike my sisters
Dead before I even understood
They were a possibility.
Some 50 years later
I still can picture
The body of my brother
Tiny, dark, dressed
As if he were going to his christening
Not his grave.
Perhaps he was the reason
I always understood
Death much better than life.
Why the dark side
Was so appealing.
They wait there, my sisters
And my brother.
Never to be, never
To have drawn so much
As one tiny breath.

Man with a Horn

Daddy was a jazzman
The old photos prove it.
There he stands, bedecked
In a bow tie, white pants
Shirt with French cuffs
Holding his trumpet, smiling slightly
Waiting to send those first, high notes
Out into the air, to be carried
On that local radio station
Whose call letters no one quite remembers.
Daddy was a jazzman
On rare occasions we would listen
To his old records, hear the greats
From the Age of Jazz
Use their music
To soar, to swoop, to have their techniques
Explained, explored, sometimes critiqued.
Daddy was a jazzman
But he never played for me.

Foretold

The dreams have become
Part of our family folklore.
Dreams of teeth
Dirty water
Babies
They all signal death.
Grandma said so.
Same as if we see
A lot of grass
Just before Christmas.
Snow will keep us safe.
Grass means someone
Will soon be giving up
The ghost.
I dreamt again
Of a baby.
Only last night
It was a girl.
Blue-eyed.
And in the background
Sat stained laundry.
If grandma were
Still with us
She would shake her head
And say
Too bad about …
Then she would fill in the name.
Someone will be
A spirit soon.
Wherever she is
Grandma lies in wait
For one of us
To join her.

Final Farewell

The ancient warrior lies silent now
Leaving his widow to her grief
His heirs to their destiny.
They hope for peace
Even though he warned them
It would never be so.
His comrades help
Lay him to rest.
Walking slowly
Facing his casket
Two by two
They snap to attention, salute
Turn on their heels
Leaving room for the next two
So fragile, so proud
Still doing their duty.
His family watches, recalling
His nocturnal demons unleashed
Wretched enough
To frighten hell's inhabitants.
Did he scream
Because of what he was forced to do
In a far-off foreign land
Or because of what was done to him?
Would the few old soldiers who remain
Explain the anguish
Or would they prefer to have
Their own battle cries
Fade into the night?
Present arms.
Fire your weapons.
Twenty-one times.
Not at the enemy
But for the ancient warrior

Who will fight no more.
His widow receives the flag
That covered his coffin.
His final war is finished.
Rest well.

And So I Came to Be

I never tired of the story
You told so many times
The story of how I came into the world.
Always glossing over
Any pain, any fear
Any doubt.
You were a natural mother
Bringing forth a life
A spirit
A part of yourself.
You said you stared in wonder
At the too long fingers
The even longer feet.
You weren't sure yet
What to call your creation.
But you always said
It was the happiest moment
In your long life.

Perhaps It is Charity

Many tried to explain the miracle
Right here, at the high priest's hand.
Do you believe?
I understand it as a gift
Of sorts
Bringing us to celebrate
An ancient ritual
Yet so common
Repeated daily
Over and over
Throughout the world.
It linked us, they said
To a community
A way to live our lives
If only we had faith
Believed the incredible stories
Handed down over the millennium.
I bow my head.
I cross myself.
I pray through the thick clouds
Of incense
And threats of hellfire
Filling the church.
Wondering what is more important
Faith
Or the hope
Someone hears me.

Naming Rights
(From the Book of Judith)

And so it came to pass
That when I was born
All the favorite names
Were already taken.
No one ever really explained
How or why I came to be called
Judith
A nice, Hebrew name.
Did anyone know
Judith was a Bible character?
A beautiful widow
She was wealthy,
Considered a good woman
By her contemporaries.
But she was called
To take up a weapon
And bring down a king.
She did what any thinking woman
Would do.
Used her beauty
And her wiles
Got herself invited
To "eat, drink and be merry."
And while her evil companion
Drank himself into oblivion
She prayed
Then struck him dead
With his own sword.
(Rumor has it
It took two tries.)
They say the head of Holofernes
Was carried off
By Judith's maid

After the lovely widow
Rolled away his headless body.
Her people triumphed
After their enemy learned
Their leader lost his head
To a comely woman.
Judith …
I hope I can
Live up to the name.

First Blood

Women stick together
It is something in our blood
That redeems us
Cleanses us
Strengthens us
Against the enemy
Be it man
Or time.
There is something feral
About so much blood
Spotting, dripping, gushing
So many ways
For life to flow
Through us
Out of us
Between us.
Watch us bleed, indeed!
Our link to our mothers
Sisters
Daughters
Begins with blood
Is sealed in bright red
Signals we are women.
It flows through our veins
Through our lifetimes.
We give birth.
We pour ourselves
Into our men, our babies
Into each other.
We whisper the secrets
Among ourselves.
It is our destiny.
It is written in
Our faded blood

Reveal Yourself

A burning bush would be nice
A voice booming from the heavens
Better still.
I want to see the lightning bolt
Watch the sun spin
Witness that guiding star
Something that would tell me
Tell us
You are here.
Why were all the good signs
Used up
On peasants
In countries far away
In centuries
Too long ago to remember?
Feel His touch in the wind, they say.
Be silent, and you will hear His voice.
I am here, I am ready to understand.
Please, could You speak up?

Questions for the Deity

Did You know
Who You were?
They say You were a prodigy
But if You knew
How could You have masqueraded
As one of us?
How could You have known
Really known
How hard, how frightening
This life was for us?
Could You feel our desperation?
I think not.
At least I do not understand
How You could have known
What it was like to be merely human
When You were so much more.
Forgive my ignorance.
If You ever knew
What true ignorance is.

Did the Devil Make Himself Do It?

What made you take that fall?
Exactly what happened
That caused you to go down in flames?
Disobedience? Jealousy?
I remember hearing those reasons.
Somehow the punishment
Doesn't seem to fit the crime.
Were you angry
Or just lonely
When you slithered up to Eve
And offered her knowledge?
Knowledge of what?
You? The truth?
Is that what evil is?
Last question.
Whatever it was
(Please whisper the answer)
Was it worth it?

Last Notes

The course schedule said it was a music
class.
Well, that sure fooled us, sitting there
Prim and proper in school uniforms
The color of mud, coupled with
Heavy stockings and clunky shoes
Guaranteed to make us look
Shapeless, hopeless
Matching the way we felt.
The old nun jabbered away, every day
For an entire year
Making that 45-minute class feel like
The eternal damnation we were
Forever threatened with.
Not one note of music was ever to be
played.
Just Sister
Going on and on about Gregorian chant
When all we wanted was some rock and roll
Heck (we didn't dare say hell)
Even a little folk music would have been
wonderful, jazz too much to hope for.
But she hummed and droned while we sat
Bored, disillusioned, staring dejectedly
Out the window
Praying (one thing we did learn)
That she wasn't really preparing us for life.

Another Sort of Dream

Youth, with all the world waiting
For my virgin feet to trod upon
Her ill-bred plains
Sighs, and cannot perceive why
I dream of death so longingly.

I am Libra

I am Libra, mistress of Aquarius
The Scales and the Water Bearer
Flowing love balanced perfectly, delicately
Never one to love the other more … or less.
It is written in our stars to be so.
Our destiny flows through the skies
Making us lovers
Making us nothing more
Than one.
Libra, mistress of Aquarius
Aquarius, lover of the deep.

Boston Hills

Some days they streak across the landscape
Slate blue, a painting, perhaps a poem
In the making.
Other days they are shrouded
Hidden so tightly in the fog
You have to believe they exist
Use blind faith to imagine
Their glorious color.
Take me there, fade with me
Into the distance.

Into the Jungle

Far too young, we were
To hear the drumbeat
The sound of boots
Boldly moving toward us.
We did not understand
Still don't
Why they came for you
And left me cold hearted
Waiting for the lover
Who would never return.
Into the jungle
Over the sand
Through the parched cities
Our husbands, our sons, now our
grandbabies
Continue the march.
They hear the distant
Cries of war.
Some go willingly
Some are taken
All to die, or worse,
Who truly understands
The crack of the rifle
The war planes screaming overhead
The staccato bursts ending
Life as we knew it?
And now we are
Far too old
To take up arms
Even if it mattered
Any more today
Than it did
So many decades ago

When you promised to return.
When I said I would wait.
There was nothing to return to
Nothing to wait for.
We were dead
Long before the last explosion
Returned us all to dust.

Promises

Indeed it is the old friends
Who nourish and nurture
Who need no explanations
No rationale, no reasons
For our being.
For our actions.
They were there from the beginning
Of our time
Stayed through the joy, the desolation
Sometimes helping to cause both
Other times smoothing it
All away.
We know they remain
In the next room, perhaps
On another continent
Ever present and aware.
Now that we have come
Nearly full circle
We make one last promise
To stay together.
We don't know yet
Who among us
Will be the first spirit
To be set free
To wait on the other side.
We don't know which one
Will lead the charge
Gain the knowledge
Stand waiting
In the next life
(Perhaps upon a cloud)
Welcoming us
Guiding us
Into an eternity

All together
Then as we are now.

Mistress Sea

I return you now
To the sea
For truly she
Is your only mistress.
I see her in your eyes
Her scent fuses
With your own
Until I am certain
It is sea water
That has mingled with your blood.
I hear her call to you
A distant thundering
In my head.
I look to see
If you, too, have heard her.
But you are already gone
Borne aloft
On a friendly wave
Reaching for a foreign shore.

3 p.m. Friday

I remember that day
Vaguely.
I wore the green and white
Striped dress
You used to say
Reminded you of an awning.
I was walking in the city
On my way to see
An old friend.
It was a hot summer day
Late on a Friday afternoon.
My friend's apartment was stifling
A sweet, powdery aroma
Filling the rooms.
What I remember more clearly
Was returning home.
You were waiting.
You lifted my hair
To help unclasp
The necklace you gave me.
I slipped out of the
Striped dress.
The smell of jasmine
Outside the window
Competed with your own
Musky scent.
I would know it
In my sleep.

Fade to Black

The old ghosts again
No longer confined
To rainy nights
And misty mornings
They now choose
To rise in daylight
Moving quickly
Despite the intense heat
At high noon.
Definitely
They are in motion!
They rise, yes
To cast their long shadows
Turning my soul
A deeper shade of gray.

Believe

I believe in life
Some state of being
After the finish
Of this time
We call death.
I believe it because
When I close my eyes
Sometimes
You return
And you appear
A bit sad.
But if I close my eyes
Tighter still
You start to smile
Then laugh.
I really think
You don't miss this world.
It misses you.

The Calling

It screams at you
What you are meant to do
Why you are here
Your raison d'etre.
Unlike the muse
Who comes and goes
Whispering in the night
Interrupting your routine
With the occasional flash of genius
This inner voice
Howls and shouts
Until you do its bidding.
You will be haunted
Ears ringing
Mind buzzing and humming
Until you give in
To what you know is true.
Is you.
It will tell you down which path
You must go.
It will push and pull you
To the blank page
The unsculpted granite
The empty canvas
Whatever awaits
Until you produce.
Only then will you
Be able to speak the truth
And say
This is my calling.

Take Me Away

Late at night
You could hear them
Coupling and uncoupling
In the still, muggy air
The trains
Filled with whatever
Needed transporting
Out of the city.
I used to imagine
How wonderful
They would be
If those trains carried passengers
Carried me
In an elegant coach
Away from the grit and grime
That gripped everything
Everyone
In this part
Of town.
My imagination carried me
Along the banks
Of the creek
That flowed at the end of the street
Right past the sign
That declared
"Dead end."
Barely moving
Its polluted stench
Overtook the hazy
Summer days
Of my youth.
I'd close my eyes
And hum "Moon River"
Pretending I could sail

Into some distant sunset.
Somewhere exotic
Somewhere, anywhere
Not here.

The Ripe Years

Across the Water

It's a vision
You, marveling at the nymphs
Dancing across the water
While spray and foam
Wash across your body.
You are laughing
In your nakedness.
The sun glares
Yet it seems to come
From within your eyes.
I wonder if you
Are going mad.
It doesn't matter.
You go into the water
And I follow.
The coral caves reveal themselves
As deep and dark.
You illuminate them.
I see the colors
Reflected in your mind.
Is it true that this life
Springs from you?
You smile and move deeper
Than I can follow.

New Love

I wonder now
At your newness
Your smile
So warm
Next to me
On the pillows.
We're talking quietly
One to the other
In the early morning light.
You ask if I am content.
No, not yet, not quite.
I do know
I am going to be with you.
I don't know how
Or why
Or for how long
But we are destined
Perhaps doomed
To remain this way
For a long, long time.

Change of Mind, Not Heart

You told me once
You loved me.
(So much nicer
Than the lovers
Who needed to remind me
They had no love to give.)
Then you very quickly
Said you take that back.
I said it was alright
You didn't know me
All that well, anyway.
And with that
I wonder
If you would be embarrassed
Or angry
If I held you to me
And told you
I think I'm beginning
To love you, too.

While You're Still Here

I'd like to hold your nakedness
Inside myself
A little while longer.
Now, this time,
My thoughts all turn to you.
It would be so good to feel
Your shoulder against my face
The touch of your back
Under my fingertips.
I want to lie next to you again,
See you smiling above me awhile longer.
Your incomparable tenderness
Weighs heavily on my mind.

Possessed

Now passionate
(Moving your hands down my body)
Now tender
(Holding my face softly in your hands)
I have found a wealth of loving
In you.
You move up
I lean forward
My fingers drawing
Needy circles
On your back.
I want you to take me
Quickly, greedily
Later to surrender
To long, slow loving
Late into the night.
How much longer
Will you make me wait
Until I can have
All of you?

Imprints in Musk

Your animal scent
Has invaded my pillow.
My covers lie bunched up
At the foot of the bed
Where you kicked them off
Before you left.
The bedspread is half on the floor
And under the bed
Since you tripped on it
This morning.
My bed has known more
Than just your form of loving.
Your body imprints
Are on the sheets.
Already there is a small gully
In the mattress
Where you have slept.
Always share my bed with me.
It knows you well.

To Dream

What do lovers dream
When they are asleep
Together
Deep in the night?
Do their dreams coincide
Or are they quite separate?
Does one remember
While the other's
Remains a soft haze?
Do they ever dream
The same thing
At the same moment?
As for me
All I want is
To sit and watch you
Lie naked to your dreams

Meditation

Sitting in a darkened room
Our mirrored reflections await Spring.
Purple candlelight
Early evening raga
Reading aloud our favorite passages
From the ancient tome.
Now and then
Our eyes meet
All you tell me
Is that when I lean forward
You can see my breasts
In the candlelight.
And they're beautiful
Ivory like.
Incense fills the air.
Outside, the rain continues.
No matter.
Morning is hours away.

Perhaps

It is quite early yet
In my time
But already
The first small, sure signs
Are upon me.
I wonder at you
Sleeping heavily next to me
You, my sometimes lover
If you have noticed at all
My fuller breasts, the gentle slope
Of my stomach, where once
It was hard and flat.
I think not, but then sometimes
I notice you watching me in a
Peculiar way, when you don't think
I see you. Other times
You softly stroke the back of my neck
Making me aware of a certain tenderness
I didn't know you possessed.
Perhaps in your silence you
Have come to realize
An heir is to be born unto you
Your wildly springing seed
Has settled within me.
I am readying for a miracle
Wondering if you are willing
To share destiny.

The Way We Weren't

Who were we then
And was there someone
Else we should have been?
Long haired and laughing
We walked the city streets
Barefoot
Dreaming of the day
We would become
Whatever it was
We were waiting for.
There was so little then.
An overheated apartment
That old third floor walkup.
Remember how we bounded up
Those flights of stairs
Flinging open windows
Wanting nothing more
Then to fall
Into each other?
Later as I brushed my hair
You would come across the room
And smile at my reflection
In the mirror.
We were young
We were in love
We were nothing, yet
To the world.
Today, the memories of Edward Street
Remind me
Of what we are not.

Old Wives Tale

She began to tell her story
Once again
In deadly detail.
I had heard it
Many times before.
But because she had
Always listened
Quietly and carefully
To my ramblings about
Other fates shared
I leaned forward
To listen, to nod
To reaffirm that yes
I knew, precisely
What she meant.
She spoke again
Of the initial disbelief.
The gradual acceptance
That was almost
But not quite … anticipation.
And in a little while
There came
Great pain
Much blood
A delirious three days
The only voices she can recall
Asking
Why did she do it.
I see the torment in her eyes.
I watch her face.
I assure her
That I believe her.
It was that wretched
"Meant to be."

Neither her will
Nor her hand
Had any cause in the matter.
She grows quiet.
She looks away.
We share the silence, the suffering
These many years cannot dull.
And the story will be repeated
By us, by others.
Women linked in phantom pains.

Mystery Child

Long before the mystics saw him
Told me, certainly,
He was to be mine
I sensed him, felt him
Hovering
Dark hair, dark eyes, smiling,
Just past my reach.
He was as real
As a child waiting to become
Something other than a spirit,
An illusion.
My man child.
Mine.

Fini

I was foolish
Thinking it could go on
And on and on
Like this forever.
I should have known
Nothing
This good would last.
Yet my mind reels
At the ending
So soon, too soon.
I wasn't finished yet
With this business
Of loving you.
How long have you
Been finished with me?

Sunset Child

Now you've shared
Your secret
The burden you've carried
From the time you left
To fight yet another war.
You left behind a child
Not by choice
Fatherhood denied you
Even as you stood
Ready to nurture
A new life.
Man up, they said
And you did
Only to be turned away.
You looked off into the distance.
Were you thinking of
Tiny fingers curled around
Your thumb?
Did you wonder
If your child shared
Your flaming hair
Easy grin
Soft, soft voice?
Strange, it is.
I thought only women
Could ache for new life
And wonder
If that child
Will hear a story of pure love.

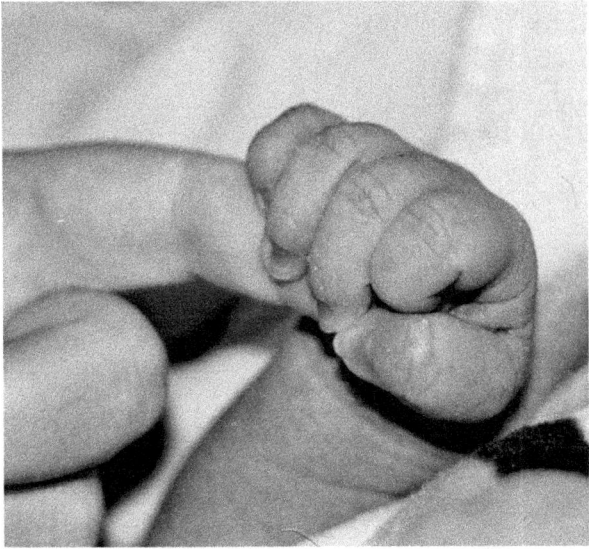

Day Heat

They were incredible days
Complete with desert lizards sunning
themselves
Heat rising out of the red clay
And me
Stretching lazily
Touching you
Waiting for the night.

Them Summer Days

We sit
Back-to-back
Like bookends
This hot summer afternoon.
I'm supposed to be
Listening to the music
Instead I'm straining
To feel your breath
Your warmth
Listening much closer
To the words you aren't saying.

This Morning

If this morning were a man
I would give myself gladly
Moving into the softness and light
I know are waiting there.
If this morning were a woman
You would take her slowly
Melting ever so gently
Into the dawn.
This morning
Is the beginning
Of a new day
A new us.
We blend together
In the pale sun
Nowhere near its zenith.

Golden

You came to me again last night
Was it just a dream
Or part of a vision
It was you, young again
Reminding me of fingers interlaced
That first, shy kiss
So many years removed
From the desperate man you became
Before the gold faded into
An explosive moment.
Do you know I mourn for you?
Do you find relief?
Is that why you return?
So that we can laugh again
When night fades into dawn
Golden with promise.

City Sunday Morning
With apologies to Tom Wolfe

The honeyed sun pours
Into the kitchen
Cleanly cutting through
The high rises.
All around us, the aroma
Of coffee
Bubbling at that certain
Percolated point.
You and I can wallow
All morning
In printers ink appliquéd
On big, fat fronds
Of today's news.
We sip the brew
Pass the paper
Back and forth
Sometimes brushing fingers.
Sunday morning in the city
You and I luxuriating
In certain torpor.

Leaving You

I'll be leaving you
I say
In five more minutes
Another hour
A year maybe
But I've yet to make
Any motion to
Really go.
I have been
Leaving you
For weeks, for months,
For years now
I've been trying
So hard
To leave you
You've yet
To let me go.

Quickly Now

London is foggy and rainy
Again today
As London is wont to be.
I say
How bloody far away
Did you say Rome is?
How many miles, how many kilometers
Are you from me?
Is Rome still as sultry
As the day I left you both?
The ringing of the wire
Pierces my own mental fog.
Your voice.
You're on your way.
Never mind the distance.
It doesn't matter.
Just hurry.

Too Late

Every time you come into me
And tell me you feel
As if you are home again
I want to hold your body
Tightly to me.
I want to give you
Everything
You should have from me, of me
In this time.
I want you
But the years have used me up.

Lost for Words

I wanted to create
Something
As wonderful
And lovely
And strong
As you.
For you.
But the words won't come.
They insist on sticking
Somewhere
In the back of my mind.
I remember them
Well enough.
And curse them
For their refusal
To be committed
To paper
Rather than just my memory.
Like us someday
They will ebb and flow.

Years Later

We wear the years well.
We have settled ourselves
And prospered quietly
Though we remain apart.
In different cities,
Other countries.
We are going to be alright
You and I.
Despite the differences.
In spite of
Because of
Each other.
Perhaps the years
Have worn us down as well.
No one has noticed
We no longer matter.

The End

She told the story
Almost joyfully
Of her final day
Of miserable bondage.
She said,
"A few dollars
A quick pound of the gavel
And we were
Officially, irrevocably
Over with."
I had to ask
"Regrets?"
She was sorry only
For all the time
They each had wasted
Knowing their time was finished
Continuing to make
So many false starts.

Omen

Such strange dreams
They are
Keeping me awake
On the far side of the bed
Making me
Break into a cold, watery sweat
And some distant pain.
I see foggy images
I pick up the scent
Of musty breath
In these peculiar nights.
Death is in the room.
I thought it was my own.
I cannot
Will not
Believe it is yours.
I awaken and find
My world shaken
Because of dreams
I cannot recall.

Antiquity

We arrange the chair just so
Hang the matching needlepoint
Just above it
Wondering where its lost twin resides.
We spoon soup out of the white tureen
Decorated with pink flowers
Now a mismatched piece
Perhaps once part of a cherished set.
How many of my ancestors did it serve?
Who brought the crystal bowls
Back from the old country
And exactly which old country was it?
They hold fruit and nuts at our holiday
celebrations
But what bounty did they once contain?
The lithographs, now,
They tell a story
Of an arranged marriage.
We don't know whose
But they have been in the family
For so many generations
They deserve a place of honor
In a parlor or a family room
Depending on the century.
The sepia of the Last Supper
Was purchased as a gift
For a grandfather's wife.
It has hung in one dining room
Or another over these many decades.
Who knows how many dinners were served
Under the ever watchful eyes
Of the Lord and his apostles.
I like all the old portraits best.
All the ancient relatives

Gone so many years.
Perhaps there are answers to my life's
questions
Hidden behind their stoic faces.
Do they wonder
Where their dishes, their crystal
Their favorite piece of furniture
Is being pressed into service?
We can only hope they feel honored
That we stay connected
Through these things
That once composed their lives.

Composite

I watch you thumb through my work.
You ask if this poem
Or that
Is about you.
I say
Guess which lover
You are.
Or were.
The lover
Who drove me
Mad with desire?
Or the one who
Simply drove me
Mad?
Was it you
I thought of
When I described
My heart's desire?
Or are you the lover
Long forgotten
In a far off
Place and time?
At this moment
I cannot recall
The color of your eyes.
And it is too late
To see for myself.

Uncherished Memory

My last clear memory of you
Is of the day, the moment
I watched you
(One bitterly cold afternoon)
Walk swiftly from the corner
Away from me
Moving effortlessly down
The crowded street.
That's the way love goes,
I guess.
Quickly, silently
Without a struggle.

Salute

So many years
Gone now
Ashes and dust
Returned to the earth.
Yet I wonder
If you know
I keep the photographs
Of you
Frozen in time
When you were young
And filled with joy.
Your mother entrusted them
To what she surely must have known
Would be my safekeeping.
Can you hear me
Across the universe
Wherever it is
You are scattered
When I face the direction
Where you last journeyed
Where you finally
Tired of your existence
And I wish you
Happy birthday.

Past Midnight

Driving through these streets
With you
Late at night
Breathing in the muggy air
I have to agree with you
I, too, am glad
We have been together
All these years
Always, it has been,
Will be
Warm and loving
This life with you.
I am glad
We have reconfirmed ourselves
In this generous night.

Need

We all know what we need
Really need
Don't we now?
If we honestly peer down
Into our souls
Or wherever it is
That our passions lurk
We know.
Most women need a mate
Who understands
That fine, crooked line
Between madness and serenity.
They need to have someone
Who understands destiny
And takes a leap of faith anyway.
Someone unafraid
To fly with them
Deep into the night.
These women need
A certain type of warlock
Someone unafraid of
Their sorcery and magic
And all that entails.
To live with the spells
These madwomen have conjured.
After all, any woman
Who howls at the moon
Needs more
Than a mere mortal
To return her feral cry.

Prov. 31, 10-31

I wanted to be that woman.
Dreamed of her
Sometimes even
Prayed to her.
You know the one.
Nameless
She brought her husband
"Good, not evil, all the days of her life."
She sounded like the perfect wife.
She sewed
She planted
And despite her sturdy arms
She wore purple well.
She was smart
And industrious.
She tended to the poor
Even while laboring
The night away
To keep her family safe and fed.
The ancient ones declared her
Kindly and wise
And a shrewd businesswoman.
"Give her a reward of her labors,"
The verses say.
Being able to laugh
At the days to come
Will suffice
For that biblical, unnamed woman.

In the Time Left

Final Task

Breathe in.
Breathe out.
Should be simple enough
While you lie back on pillows
Staring at the ceiling
With nothing else left to do.
We cannot reach you
Only wonder
If you are somewhere
High above the semi-darkness
The rest of us occupy.
Perhaps you are
Watching, waiting, listening to us.
Now you know the answers to all the
questions,
The life-long mysteries we have pondered.
But you aren't letting on.

Child of Illusion

Who is she
This woman who comes to visit
Wearing the same black dress
Standing in the same place?
Day and night
She haunts your dreams
Or is it your reality?
You question her ghost.
She is your first born.
She does not exist.

Quarter Moon

There it is again
That silvery sliver of moon
Hanging there
Reminding me
Of those sad little quarter moons
Etched on your hospital gown.
The pattern creator
Must have thought
"How clever this is."
I knew the first time I saw them
I would never be able to view
A quarter moon again
Without being dissolved in pure grief.
Without wondering if somewhere
You, too, are watching
And waiting
For your loved ones
To see that little piece
Of moon
From the other end
Of the night sky.

Dreams of the Dead

Do the dead dream?
How long before their souls
Find their way to whatever
Final resting place awaits them?
When do the mysteries unfold?
Is there a moment when all knowledge
Is there, like a flash?
Is that the white light
We are urged to enter?
If the dead do dream
They dream of us.

Final Resting Place

We all tend to the gardens
Of the dead
In our own way.
Trees and flowers
Flags and wreaths
All find a way
To pay their respects.
A friend once told me
He takes two cans of beer
To the cemetery
Leans against his father's headstone
And talks to him
Trusting he will hear
If only in his soul
The answers he needs.
It's the old folks
Who can break your heart
Watching them lean against
A mausoleum stone
Singing "Happy Birthday"
To a loved one long gone.
Seeing them lie in wait
For other mourners
Just for the momentary relief
Of having someone to talk to.
Are cemeteries for the dead
Or the living?
They are the places
Where dreams go to die.

Query to the Spirits

Is it possible for a spirit
On its final journey
To pass through the soul
Of its own creation?
I was so certain, at that moment, I felt your
life
Pass through me
Leaving me
Bitter with the knowledge
You chose to take flight
In solitude.
Or was this your final farewell
A lasting gift to carry me
To the end of my own story?

Mirror, Mirror

You hold up the mirror
To friends and enemies alike
Although in your twisted mind
They've all become the same.
Their faults and flaws reflected back
On them.
At you.
You try
Oh how you try
To diminish, to demean
To gouge them all with shards of broken
glass.
It is your image that is shattered
Beyond recognition
Beyond reason.
Have you seen yourself?
Hold up the broken mirror.

And Back to You

Your tongue was like a serpent's
Hissing and spewing
So many poisons
No one left your inner circle
Unscathed.
Years of dripping acid
Hotly into your people's wounds
Has left you with no one
To absorb the venom.
I hope you get
All that you deserve.
Is that is a blessing
Or a curse?

City Love

We were like
Children again
At least I felt
Like a young girl
Rather than a woman
Too old to be
Sitting in a dark cafe
Holding hands in the street
Exchanging kisses
In the square.
We did all the romantic things
We used to do
So many years ago.
And now, again,
You have taken your leave.
Unlike the young girl
Who used to be left feeling
Terribly lonely for you
The woman in me
Is satisfied.

A Good Place to Grow Up

The old, red brick house
Is up for sale
A bargain, perhaps
For the right person
Or family, maybe.
Two bedrooms, one bath
Living room, dining room
Kitchen facing the garden
(Slash pet cemetery)
Describes the house
But doesn't' tell the entire story.
There's a loft
Where many intimate conversations were
had
Over many bottles of wine.
Countless holidays were celebrated
So much food served
Around the antique dining table
To family and friends
To anyone who needed a place to be.
There is a perfect spot for a Christmas tree
In the living room
That was carved out
Of what once served
As the master bedroom.
And the kitchen
That kitchen!
So small, so full
Of the scent
Of coffee percolating
And old world cooking.
Here, here is the heart of this old house!
There are nooks and crannies and great
Hiding places.

Perhaps even a ghost or two.
If you listen closely
You can hear a family, complete with a dog
Birds, fish
Gathered close
Laughing, changing, growing old.
There are nicks in the woodwork
Some scratches on the paint
Touches of real people
Living their lives.
It was home.

Talk to Me

That tired drawl
Lingers still
Like a tongue
Moving sweetly
Around an ear.
How many years
Since you last whispered
"Talk to me"?
(I imagine the lines
That must now be etched
Deeply around your eyes.
They make you
Only dearer to me.)
And so I will
Talk to you
And hope my worn words
Still warm you
In the night.

You, Young

Late last night
I saw someone
Who reminded me
Of you
When you were young.
I watched his animal moves
Heard his laughter
Open and teasing.
I wanted to take his face
Into my hands
And kiss him softly.
It was you
Before your eyes
Grew tired lines
Around them.
You
Before the world wore you out.
I turned from him
As the ache of wanting you
Tore me open
Once again.

On Aging Well

You could have had
The decency
To have gotten
Fat around the middle
Or at the very least
Lost some hair.
As soon as I saw that photo
I knew it was you.
Unwrinkled, unblemished
Still those perfect teeth.
I held your image
Next to an old photo
I had saved.
Four decades have passed
Since we stood together
In front of a camera
Our youth caught
Forever on film.
Sometimes when I look
At that old photo
I remember
Being in love
That Sunday
That summer.
I can only guess
At what happened to you
Never really knowing
What path you chose
What life you made
For yourself, or
For someone else.
I can only hope
You are in love
Even if it's not with me.

Among My Souvenirs

Here they sit
Waiting for my attention
Poems I have written
A gold chain
Dried flowers
Pressed into a book.
Gifts from an old love?
An embarrassment of riches, indeed!
I can no longer remember
The lover
Who pushed back my hair
And fastened the gold chain
Around my neck.
Could he have been the same one
To whom I wrote the poems?
Was it he
Who gave me the book
Or the flowers?
Was it one man
Or many?
I don't recall the lovers …
Just the love.

Into the Shadows

I believed your spirit
Would be gone
By now.
I thought the journey
Was finished
So long ago.
Yet I still feel
You here
Breathing behind the walls
Moving in the darkness
I've come to know.
So close, I can almost
Touch you.
I feel your shadow near me.
It is heavy.
Is it as difficult
For spirits
To let go
As it is
For mere mortals?

How Many, Really?

Exasperated, you ask
Just how many centuries
Have you known me
Really?
So many
Too many
To count in human time.
We flew together in the night
Sometimes toward each other
Other times away
And yes,
There were times
We drew blood.
They say people do that, too
You know.
Poor creatures.
We never did
Quite understand them.
Something to do
With our being
One and only
With and without
Each other.
Sometimes it all
Felt like a riddle.
Perhaps someday we will say
Mystery solved.
We will look back
Over all those lifetimes
Counting and recounting
Starting with the ancient hours
When the world was new
And ending
Somewhere.

Yellow Bird

Are there really omens?
Or do we assign meaning
Where none exists?
I opened the window shade
Early this morning
And there it was.
A small, yellow bird
Walking across the patio.
It stayed for just a moment
Then took flight.
Your favorite bird.
Your favorite song.
Was it a sign that
You are with me?
You said that when you went
To your heavenly reward
You wanted the job
Of feeding the birds.
Perhaps this was
One of your charges
You sent along
To grant me comfort
In these troubled times
One small
Yellow bird.

The Last Time

If we knew it was the last time
We were to touch, to kiss
To see each other in this lifetime
Would we have held on a little longer
Kissed more tenderly
Turned around one more time
To watch our mutual retreat?
Or would we have waited
Trying to keep time
And space and distance
At bay
Holding on to the belief
There would be another time.
Perhaps we would have unleashed our
passion
Our longing
Disregarded any thought
We could not go on forever.

About the Author

Judith A. Rucki grew up in Cheektowaga, a Buffalo, N.Y. suburb known for its hardworking blue-collar families who were the backbone of the community.

Since she was a child, Judith always enjoyed writing, especially poetry. But being the practical sort, she earned a B.S. in Business Administration from the University at Buffalo and a M.S. in public relations management from Buffalo State College. She also attended Cornell University's School of Labor and Industrial Relations.

Most of her 40+-year career was spent in marketing, advertising and public relations along with a stint as an adjunct professor at Buffalo State.

She currently resides in Bowmansville, another suburb of Buffalo. These days she is indulging her love of poetry and writing with an occasional trip into the kitchen to cook and bake.

Anyone in need of public relations counsel or freelance writing can contact her at ruckija@gmail.com.